Don't Judge M

I'm A Single Parent!

DEDICATION AND APPRECIATION

This book is dedicated to all single parents working hard daily to ensure they fulfil their roles in the lives of their children.

It has also been written as a source of encouragement to many who are on the verge of giving up, or those who think they have failed in their roles, encouraging them to persevere, to be strong, find help and also receive the grace to always deliver.

Firstly, I want to thank my God for strengthening me throughout this season and up till now. I never thought I would have the time to write as I had to deal with many other issues of life. However, the Lord saw me through in the midst of it all; therefore I give him the glory, honour and praise. Indeed! He made it possible.

I would also like to thank my children for their love and support, and for being obedient and submissive as children, even when they did not feel like it. They have made it easier for me to perform my parental duties through the years. I also want to appreciate them for their roles in the writing of this book, especially through motivation by my daughter Doris, and my son Franklyn who helped me with both technical and administrative formalities.

My next set of appreciations go to my editor Deacon Jennifer Oluwalana, who spent countless days and weeks to ensure things went well, and also to my spiritual father, mentor, and teacher Pastor Boomy Tokan who first encouraged me to write, which is not something I ever saw myself doing. He saw the good in me that I could not see, and for this reason he kept encouraging me until the very end. His work behind the scenes has been excellent. I also extend my gratitude to his wife Mrs Charline Tokan for her contribution in perfecting the "loose ends" on this book and also for her tremendous encouragement that "I can do it".

I also want to appreciate Deacon Naomi Adotey and Jacinta Egbuchue for their endless support from beginning to the end, constantly monitoring my progress day in day out, followed on with prayers on my behalf. A massive thank you goes out to leaders and disciples at my church, most of who have been with me from the beginning of my journey.

Great appreciations go to my father, siblings and extended family for their tremendous support through the years. I could not have done it on my own.

To the family of my late husband, I say a huge thank you for being there for myself and the children.

To my friends, associates and many more that this space cannot contain, I appreciate you all for your immeasurable support and contributions whether it's a joyous occasion or a sad one, you have been there.

Finally, I extend my appreciation to everyone who has supported my family in every way be it through childcare, spiritual advice, financial gifts, emotional and social support through this journey of survival and thriving. There is a common saying that "It takes a community to raise a child." I can honestly say that I have experienced that in raising my children and having a hand in raising other children too.

TABLE OF CONTENTS

INTRODUCTION

According to the Collins English Dictionary, single parent is defined as a person who has a: *'Dependent child or dependent children and who is widowed, divorced, or unmarried.'*

Unfortunately, I found myself in the category of being "widowed" having lost my husband in 2009 due to illness. Other single parents might be in the category of divorced, separated or unmarried.

In this book, I will be touching on the following topics; my own previous perception of single parenting, the challenges of caring and providing emotional, financial and other necessary support for my children. I will also touch on dealing with stigma and self-esteem issues, and the mechanisms I used to overcome on a daily basis, followed by a celebration of the amazing work done by single parents, some life lessons and inspirational quotes.

I have added some biblical scriptures as a source of hope and encouragement, and guidance for those who might be looking for Godly counsel and perhaps do not actually know how and where or what to look for.

The Word of God was one of the greatest tools I used and found the purpose of it very fulfilling, and how relying on it helped me through the years. This also gave me the courage and boldness to share my story with many. I have also shared other single parents' views and experiences to help my readers see similarities across the board.

CHAPTER 1

My Years of Growing Up

I grew up back home in Sierra Leone in West Africa. I was brought up by both parents and fully provided for until I graduated from university. My siblings and I have been blessed and contented without any complains. We had enough to the point that my mother would give to some of our neighbours who were in need. I could vividly remember how I stole food stuff and other things just to give to some of my mates who were in need. We lived a very blessed life for a typical African family. My father was in the military and my mother was a teacher. They both progressed in their careers and achieved highly. Despite loving us, they also disciplined us. I could vividly remember how they never spared us from punishments. For example, using the whip on us was part of our daily lives. We also had a great social life. Our parents would introduce us to every aunty and uncle until we lost count. My dad was good at organising family outings where we connected and networked with other families and also got to meet their children. Life was great and it was like that for many years of our growing up. However, there comes a time in life when people go through life's challenges, so my parents went through theirs every now and then. But by the grace of God, they overcame.

I remembered during the late 90's how things became a bit tough for us as a family, due to my dad being in prison and awaiting death by hanging; also thanking God for availing on his behalf as he was later granted amnesty alongside other inmates by the government. We were very strong together as a unit, and also aided by prayer and the unlimited grace of God, we were not depleted. Our parents continued to support my siblings and I until we all got married, and one by one moved out to settle with our spouses. That was the typical way of an African upbringing, schooling, sixth form, university and marriage. In those days, all other means of education was classed as low standard.

My Previous Perception of Single Parenting

After university, I got married to my husband who has passed on as mentioned earlier. I had my dreams and expectations like any young married person could have. Also, having been brought up in a well-structured setting, I was oblivious to things such as single parenting, even though I had witnessed my schoolmates losing either or both parents, or parents gone through divorce or separation, or young ladies being dumped by men after impregnating them. I witnessed all of this but just did not pay any attention to it; maybe because I was not directly affected at the time and not having been in their situation. My oblivion continued.

We got married and I relocated to London, United Kingdom, where I started building up my own family with my late husband. Everything was a total shock to me, and it took me years to assimilate into the culture and way of doing things. Understanding the British way of education and discipline, the welfare system, tolerance and diversity; just too many to take in as this was completely different to the way things were done in Sierra Leone. I had to give things a try day by day once I started having my children.

One thing that was very obvious and I kept asking questions about was "why so many mothers around and also fathers pushing babies around on buggies, especially mothers with so many children around them?" Then all I used to hear was so many single parents around just living on benefits, or having children because they wanted a house, or trying to reap as much as they can from the government. What never crossed my mind was the fact that many of these parents did not just find themselves in this situation of being single parents. Something must have led to their singleness; also ignoring the fact that parents go through divorce, separation and loss of a spouse. I was carried away with the flow of mostly negative news about single parenting, not going to work, buying expensive things for their children, living way beyond their means and ending up in debt and losing their homes for not catching up with rent arrears or neglect of property. Another common saying about single parents was their use and abuse of drugs, neglect of children whereby social services often gets involved, and children being placed into care.

A lot of what I used to hear had an impact on the way I viewed single parents being male or female. My pastor once preached on the impact of what we hear whether positive or negative, and how it can affect us. What we hear constantly, we will end up believing. Once believed, it can be hard to change except one opens their minds to flexible reasoning. As I speak now, these issues still exist but I came to realise that this was not an issue with single parents only, though they may be among the majority. Some of the issues highlighted can exist in fully fledged families too. It felt like society had presented a lot more negative than positive views on this "topic", and sadly it felt like a lot of people, including myself, were so quick to judge and make wrong accusations of which we have no proof.

> *"Do not judge, or you too will be judged. For in the same way you*

judge others, you will be judged,
and with the measure you use, it
will be measured to you."
Matthew 7:1-2

There is also another popular saying that "*one should not judge a book by its cover*". This simply means one has to know and understand someone's situation before making up their mind about them. I also learnt as time went on that every single parent has a reason for their singleness, therefore, I cannot put them all in the same category. They all go through similar challenges but through diverse ways.

I can testify to this, having had this experience through the years, hence my courage to write about this.

My Real Deal of Experiences

I previously mentioned about the loss of my husband, and I would say that prior to his departure, my role as a single parent had already started. I was taking care of my husband and the children by doing the school runs, cooking, activities, and obviously my spiritual duty never left untouched as this kept me going. It almost seems as if the Lord was preparing me for such a time like this, little did I know it then. For He is the all-knowing God (omniscient), the Alpha and Omega, the Beginning and the End. What I could not foresee, God already knew. I would say even though my husband was terminally ill, I still had high expectations for a miracle. With this in mind, I refused to think that I would end up on my own. Well, faith kept me going as that was what I had. Someone might say that was not a very realistic point of view, but that is how I chose to stand in the situation.

My husband passed on and then the reality that I would be the sole carer of my children sank in very deeply. I said to myself "Floris, you have already been doing it." My husband was still around and would manage to do a few things where strength permitted, so I still appreciated that. But now, I was on my own. On MY OWN! It was 'me, myself and I'. I asked myself 'how am I going to cope?' In a land where my mother was not physically present; most of us know and understand the roles of grandparents in the lives of their grandchildren. Europe was completely different to Africa where one can receive so much physical, emotional and financial support. In addition, there is extended family. I know that some individuals do enjoy such support, but this was something I lacked at the time. However, I still had support from my wonderful church, my sister in-law and family, I had my younger sister and husband too, as well as some great friends who I would rather address as sisters. They were a true reflection of this popular adage "sometimes water is thicker than blood." 'Simply' means the Lord lets us encounter people that we are not related to, but end up creating a very big positive impact on our lives. Some people are just there for you regardless. I had to really appreciate my Lord for His kindness and favour towards me. However, I still had to deal with the reality being the sole carer of my children due to those people having to tend to their own responsibilities. This made it necessary for me to manage my expectations of them.

I would like to take this opportunity to thank everyone for their love, support, giving of their time and resources, and just being there for my family. I cannot reiterate this statement that "it is a community that raises a child". I also thank my

Lord daily for the help he sent me during my trying times. He never left me neither forsook me, though I felt like He did sometimes.

Prayer:

> "May the Lord answer you when you are in trouble; may He send you help from the sanctuary and sustain you from Zion. O Jesus, when thou pleadest for us in our hour of trouble, the Lord Jehovah will hear thee." **Psalm 20:1**

For assurance and comfort:

> "Be strong and courageous. Do not be afraid or terrified because of them, for the LORD your God goes with you; he will never leave you nor forsake you." **Deuteronomy 31:6**

CHAPTER 2

Single Parenting and Mental Health

Going through the daily routine, knowing that you are on your own, for most of the time, can be very daunting for our state of mind. Statistics show that the average single parent gets depressed on several occasions especially when financial and other needs of the family cannot be met. Below is an article on research that was carried out by the "Metro" in March 2018 showing us some statistics:

> [1]*"Raising a family is a dream for many of us, but the picture-perfect image of a two-parent household is actually a lot less common than you might think. In fact, there are about 2 million single parents in the UK, which makes up nearly a quarter of families with dependent children. If raising kids as part of a dynamic duo is difficult then going solo is a job which undoubtedly requires extra support, and this couldn't be more important for single parents with*

---

[1]

https://metro.co.uk/2018/03/03/these-single-parents-tell-us-what-its-like-to-live-with-depression-while-raising-kids-7344105/

depression. Statistics suggest that about 68% of women and 57% of men with mental health problems are parents, and the most common mental health problems experienced during pregnancy and after birth are anxiety, depression and post-traumatic stress disorder. It's not just women who are at risk either, with about 10% of all new fathers worldwide experiencing postnatal depression. Single mothers are more likely to experience poor mental health than those with a partner, and the main causes associated with this are the financial hardships as well as a lack of social support. The research also gives us opinions expressed by some single mothers."

I would really encourage you to check out the full article, and I am sure that many of us can relate.

Some parents struggle to put food on the table, at least a decent meal, also not able to buy school uniforms, not to talk about free school dinners, as not everyone is qualified to receive it. A lot of single parents cannot afford the expenses of extra-curricular activities, such as school trips and other outings etc. What about holidays or the normal treats of clothes shopping, sorting out childcare and balancing with work etc? The majority of single parents cannot afford any extras.

I can testify to most of what is listed above, though as time went by, things got a little better as the Lord helped me identify some extra skills which boosted my income. However, things were still proving challenging, and just going through that torture everyday was not an easy journey to go through. Many single parents go to bed and wake up in the morning with the burden of managing to get by.

Having said all of this, there are still other single parents who can afford the above for their children, but still go through depression for other reasons. That is the reason why everyone cannot be classified into the same category as stated earlier. I have personally witnessed both single mums and dads go through emotional abuse by their ex-partners, some to the extent of physical abuse. Using emotional and mental manipulation and not contributing towards the child because dad is upset with the mother is a very common scenario in society these days. Separated mothers not showing up when it is their turn to have the children, probably upset as dad is now married or dating another woman or vice versa. This manipulation has the tendency to cause so much emotional damage especially when the children are caught up in between, not realising the damage it causes to the children. This is a situation, if not managed properly, that can also be used by the children against the opposite parent.

Though my other half is not alive, I had situations where my children would often compare me to their late dad. My son was good at this as each time he was refused something he wanted me to buy for him, he would then say to me that his dad would have bought it anyways, if he was still alive. This would just get me angry. My response would be; "not necessarily so son". I have also witnessed and heard of similar stories where children would seize every opportunity they have to play with their parent's minds, this is also experienced in intact families too. This shows me that the emotional battles can range from the simplest to the most complex of issues.

Coping Mechanisms

I made a decision that I had to keep my mind in check, by deciding what I could allow into my mind and ears both from inside and outside forces. I decided I had to be there for my children regardless, that I was not going to let issues get through to weigh me down to the point of destruction. I just finished reading a book by Dr Caroline Leaf, "Switch on Your Brain", and one of the things she highlighted in her book was "the power of what we hear or allow to rest in our thoughts". This means if we do not manage negative situations well, they will take control of our entirety. Negativity can impact our entire outlook about life and the way we deal with

situations. On the other hand, positivity can cause greater impact and also produces much better results. Therefore, it means that whatever situation we find ourselves in, we must try by all means to have control over our minds, think about some positive things that can come out of that situation, which also gives some peace of mind. Thinking positively helps us find solutions to problems. It also gives us hope that all is not lost.

In the beginning, all I saw about my situation with my children was "all hope lost" and that was it. I did not make any room for flexible thinking. A lot of us do this every now and then. I lost the joy of motherhood as I thought I would never cope being alone. My emotions were all over the place. I was so stressed because I thought I was stuck, and that my life was a "yoyo", or just going into circles doing the same things over and over again. This is where I was then, and I do believe a lot of us have been there at some point. I decided to take control back; the willpower to live for my children, regardless and to deal with every battle of the mind. I was dealing with the death of my husband and at the same time trying to care for my children. I asked myself this question; who is looking after me then? Those going through single parenting due to separation and other reasons might have their own questions too. I was overwhelmed. I never used to visit the GP surgery, but I soon faced the reality that I needed to do so due to uncontrollable headaches. The kind of headaches I had then were on another level. They were one-sided, sometimes it felt like my head was about to split into two. I got told by my GP this was due to stress. I remembered arguing with her that I was not stressed. I was prescribed a medication for the headaches and also another that was to help with muscle relaxation. I was adamant to take the second medication due to opinions about taking such medications and the side effects they could have. God bless my pastor's wife, who was also a medical consultant. She had to sit me down and explain things for me to understand where I was and the help I needed. I had no option but to yield to her counsel since she knew what she was talking about, and also wanted the best for my sanity. I was on the medications for a while, and stopped them gradually as things got better. I realised that both professionals meant no harm at all. It was all for my good.

Stress is not a topic of discussion for many especially for men. It almost seems like it is an abomination to talk about it. We need to face the fact that stress is a killer if not dealt with. In addition, if not dealt with, this affects both parent and child dynamics in the home which now translates to life outside of home. Quite a few children are in care, and statistics show us almost 50% of the children in care are from single parent homes. Bottom line is issues have erupted and proper coping mechanisms have not been put in place.

Seeking Help - Counselling

Help is always at hand and therefore our responsibility to make the most of every opportunity by reaching out and make use of what is available. The idea of counselling was not popular then, but now one of the best ways available to society, providing a variety of services to individuals struggling to cope with various issues in life. Professional counsellors work in confidential settings with individuals who are experiencing personal difficulties, to help them overcome their problems and to make appropriate changes to their lives.

The challenge some individuals have is that they feel ashamed of talking about their shortcomings, either because there is the feeling of failure, or the issue of trusting the person they speak to. Most counsellors we encounter might not be people that we know or meet on a daily basis. My candid advice is to seek help by finding a counsellor to talk to. Do not be anxious about the likelihood of losing your children to social services. Social services can only get involved in the life of a family where there is a suspicion of safeguarding issues. Also the process is always very long except for extreme cases. My advice is, let us not be too quick to pass judgement on ourselves. Help is always at hand to see us through life's challenges.

Religious Counselling

This type of counselling can be given by a spiritual leader, in the person of a pastor/reverend etc. found in a place of worship, sometimes outside of church too. A God-fearing individual who is not a leader, but has respect in the community can also be approached by individuals for counselling. Seeking religious counselling can be slightly different, as not only will the spiritual leader give advice and signposting, he or she will also endeavour to pray for the person seeking help. The word of God is always used to help with whatever situation there might be. Some might also advise deliverance exercises and suggest times for fasting. A major benefit from your spiritual leader is the support one can get both emotionally and spiritually because of the relationship that already exists in some instances. One is bound to receive support especially if you are actively serving in your local church community, unless there is a situation of not opening up and no one knows about the situation.

I can testify of how spiritual counselling helped me greatly in the various life struggles I have been through. I must applaud my leaders and my local church family, and also many other men and women of God not in my present assembly, but who have been there for me through the years. I believe in showing appreciation to people who have been there for you.

I have laid this option here just for us to know that there are various avenues available to us when we need help. We are not to be in isolation and end up suffering on our own. Others are there to carry on with us as we pass through until we get through to the brighter side of life.

Prayer

This is another powerful coping mechanism. For those of us who are practising believers, I trust you must be used to this. Just going to your Father when you cannot take it anymore, or when you feel it is too much, when you need direction or trusting Him to send you help and connecting you to the right people. Praying and seeking His face regarding the children, when it feels like the children are going astray, or being extremely disobedient, seeking for peace and joy when broken-hearted, or when feeling so low. When you are trusting Him on how a provision is going to be made to put food on the table for your children, how the next uniform shopping will be done, and the list can go on, and on and on.

Prayer has been a pivotal part of my life journey. My faith kept me going despite all odds, with doubts kicking in sometimes, but I am grateful to my Father for his grace. It has been part of me to communicate with my father, sometimes just dumping all my burdens on his shoulder. Also convinced of what he said here in **Matthew 11:28**;

> *"Come to me, all you who are weary and burdened, and I will give you rest. Take my yoke upon you and learn from me, for I am gentle and humble in heart, and you will find rest for your souls. For my yoke is easy and my burden is light."*

His word tells us that we can come to Him and present our petitions and just believe that He is able to answer us because we seek Him. I found **Philippians 4:6** very helpful too. It reads;

> *"Do not be anxious about anything, but in every situation, by prayer and petition, with thanksgiving, present your requests to God."*

Hebrews 4:16 is also one of my assurance scriptures. It reads;

> *"Let us then approach God's throne of grace with confidence, so that we may receive mercy and find grace to help us in our time of need."*

> *"Cast all your anxiety on Him because He cares for you."* **1 Peter 5:7**

> *"So do not fear, for I am with you; do not be dismayed, for I am your God. I will strengthen you and help you; I will uphold you with my righteous right hand"* **Isaiah 41:10**

There are times when the going really gets tough and it can feel like there is no hope for the future. Scriptures like **Jeremiah 29:11-13** come in very handy to give you hope for the future. It reads;

> *"For I know the plans I have for you," declares the Lord, plans to prosper you and not to harm you, plans to give you hope and a future. Then you will call on me and come and pray to me, and I will listen to you. You will seek me and find me when you seek me with all your heart."*

Wow! I can go on and on with the comfort and strength that I have received in the Word and in prayer. This has done my soul very well and still does.

There are also other types of spiritual mechanisms such as deep meditation, exercises etc. It shows that there are various positive ways to cope. However, the choice is left with us whether we want to choose positively or negatively.

Sharing Ideas

Sharing ideas with others does not make one any less a person. As single parents, it is beneficial for us when sharing ideas. It is easier to find out how your own dynamics work compared to other parents. Parents can also find out how to draw ideas or even learn from each other. I discovered that my way of caring for my children can be slightly different from how other parents do theirs. I believe there is always room for improvement. We cannot have a closed mind on talking to one another as single parents. It will amaze us how one's story can inspire and encourage others to keep going. It might be asking other parents how they coped with their teenagers, or coping without their partners, coping with school runs, child-minding, finance, working/business, personal development, feeding and general welfare issues.

Knowing my African background and the kind of mentality I had previously would have prevented me from interacting with others. However, most of us are privileged to find ourselves in environments where we are free to talk despite the circumstances at hand.

I am stressing this mostly for male single parents, who are struggling simply because of their inner pride as men, refusing to relate with others as this can be deemed shameful or weak in their mind. I am also very conscious of the fact that this affects a lot of Afro-Caribbean men. The good news is this; there is a saying that no man or woman should suffer as a result of their circumstances. There are many avenues to resolving issues. I have also learnt that one of the ways to cope with situations is to use all means available to deal with that situation. As a single parent, there are times when I looked around and saw other single parents thinking that they were all perfect, and the only difference was that they lacked partners. However, that perspective was quickly changed once I was opportune to have a conversation with them. I sometimes had to take a very deep breath before responding. It also happens the other way round when other parents speak to me. Hmm! It's amazing the stories we hear from one another. Therefore, we will fail ourselves if we judge so quickly. Talking to one another encourages, and also makes us know we are not alone, that many others are in the same situation too.

> *"Therefore encourage one another and build each other up, just as in fact you are doing".*

1 Thessalonians 5:11

I hardly come across support/networking groups for single parents. Is it because of the stigma surrounding this? Are single parents themselves ready to stand boldly and confidently? Such questions come to mind. Until such barriers are broken, those of us in that position might have to forcefully find a way to interact with others. Maybe during the school runs, at the park, at parties, community events, benefits office, housing office, council offices, at the GP surgery, restaurants; all these venues create the opportunities for mums and dads to have conversations. To cut it short, where there is a will, there's a way indeed.

Below is an extract from the same research done by "Metro" in March 2018, whereby some of the mums spoke about how they sought for help:

> *"Amy adds. 'You need support and need to reach out for that'. The first step should always be talking to someone you trust, as well as your GP who can provide you with*

professional advice and support groups in your area. Ellen revealed what's helped her the most and she said: 'Medication. I wanted to speak to a therapist then I had to self-refer. 'I am also lucky that my parents are supportive and help out where they can'. Mum Kelly says talking to other single parents is a lifeline: a way to make friends and a safe space to talk. 'I make a conscious effort to reach out and broaden my social network so that I have as much support as I can and to spend time with people in similar situations. That helps massively. 'I go to mental health charities and counselling when I can find it too' With friendly support, medical help and giving yourself a break now and again managing depression alongside the job of being a single parent is achievable."

As I previously mentioned, there are several ways to seek help. Try them all and stick to what is best for you.

CHAPTER 3

Dealing with Societal Stigma

Stigma means a strong feeling of disapproval that most people in a society have about something, It can also mean a mark of disgrace associated with a particular circumstance, quality, or person. Other synonyms are shame, disgrace, dishonour, stain, taint, blemish, etc.

Nowadays, it seems to be that the above mentioned synonyms are frequently associated with being a single parent. We might need to ask ourselves whether some of the labelling or stigmas placed by society are fair. Afterwards, one might want to bring up other situations like cheating, divorce and domestic violence. These can also be considered as a shame, disgrace and honour, but most often, amongst family only and sometimes amongst religious communities. It's amazing how such topics are easily swept under the mat. Obviously, single parenting would always be in the limelight as it has to do with the social welfare system on a larger scale.

Here are some of the most common stigmas/stereotypes.

Common Stigmas or Stereotypes

For the past 8 years of me being a single mother, I can openly confess that if I did not have a strong mind, self-will and determination, I would have suffered greatly from self-esteem issues. I have always asked myself this question: why do I find myself in this situation? But on the other hand, I am also quick to find an answer, that also reminds me that I never planned it, that situations happen and life does not stop there but moves on. Also, I am not the only person going through the same situation.

I have noticed that single parents suffer the most from societal stigma these days. In previous years, stigma was around individuals suffering from HIV. Though there are many other issues that will normally warrant stigma, they tend to slide down easily. However, with single parenting, that has not been the case. Just the sound of it when mentioned always seems to mean something negative in the minds of the media, government, which now transcends to the society. Those words "single parent" seem to carry so much weight/baggage. It also attracts so much attention, maybe due to the way it's being presented.

I have experienced on several occasions the facial expressions that individuals make when I tell them that I am single. Obviously, some are sometimes curious and just want to know why, or some don't continue with the discussion especially if they feel embarrassed to ask. On the other hand, some individuals immediately respond by making comments such as; wow! I know it is not easy for you, or keep up the good work, or more grace to your elbow, (meaning the lord help you or give you extra strength) knowing that it takes double work and effort to raise children by oneself. I could understand why people feel this way, but what surprised me was other insensitive questions that some individuals would ask or comments they would make such as; "why are you not finding a man that will help you?" I know two heads are better than one, but that's not the case for everyone. If we are to be true to ourselves, there are some households where the dynamics can be very different, and we hear stories of fathers not doing their part in terms of supporting their families properly, sometimes even mothers, although the latter is less common. So there is no guarantee that having a partner will be the definite solution to receiving support. Some single parents have actually decided that it is better for them to run their homes on their own as it is much better for them despite challenges. I am not saying this is the right order, but again, I have to respect people's choices, not forgetting that the reasons behind someone ending up single are varied.

If someone came out of their relationship due to a terrible violence, it might take them years to trust and allow someone else into their lives, as they might have to deal with and overcome all the fears, worries and anxieties before venturing into another relationship. The individual might have so many thoughts going on in their minds as to whether it's worth trying again with a new relationship. Also, some parents prefer the lone parent status in order to maintain some stability for their children, also avoiding further issues that can cause emotional damage to the child or children.

Bowing down to relationship pressures can cause damages entirely. Society needs to be considerate and not put lone parents under pressure, but let processes take their course.

Another encounter I have often had with individuals is when I attend events and am seated on a table with couples. I often get asked this question; where is your husband? With no disrespect to our African elders, and also middle-aged, this kind of practice is common. I also noticed that this is common amongst women. Why? Well, some of us might argue that this is due to some form of insecurity on the part of us women. How can a beautifully dressed or attractive woman be seated amongst or mingling with couples in general? Well, I believe it is normal to have such feelings about people.

I was once a wife and I could remember having such sentiments when I saw my husband making himself very comfortable with women in general, more so if they were single. It is a normal feeling to have, except for some extreme cases. One thing that I have always done is to smile while I respond to such questions about my partner or husband. It almost feels like it is a tag-along. Sometimes it feels like it is a must (still that same vibe of societal pressure), making a single person feeling guilty, as though it is a crime to be single. Such pressures and unnecessary expectations put on individuals has landed many in the ditch, ending up in physical and emotional abuse. It is obviously great to have a partner and work together. On the other hand, not having the right one can have serious consequences. Let's watch out!

Another common stereotype is that single mothers are "slags". A slag is a woman who has many casual sexual encounters. I kept wondering why on earth 'should one be tagged in this way?' My other question is;' what about the men?' It almost seems like it is normal thing for the men and yet, they are not tagged in this way. It seems that women go through a lot of societal stigmas than men. I feel people go into relationships, hoping it will turn out well, but in the end they split up, then move on to another relationship in the hopes that it will be successful, only to find themselves alone again. It can go on and on like a vicious circle. Some individuals do not often pause and reflect to see where they need to make some necessary changes. The end result is a lot of individuals especially women, finding themselves in this merry go-round situation. I do not want to believe individuals deliberately plan their lives to be this way. There is also a psychological aspect to this, and sadly again women find themselves in this situation. Emotions do fly all over the place when it comes to women, due to the various issues they go through in life and the way we are 'wired'. Some women feel it is a must that they be in a relationship; like it is the only way out. Some women are vulnerable and sometimes end up in the hands of men who take advantage of them too. I have heard of many abuse stories. Obviously, if someone is high on drugs, sleeping rough, and sometimes living in sheltered housing, they are bound to become vulnerable. Depression is also key in situations like this. When a woman is down, a thousand and one things are going on in her mind. All they need is a shoulder to cry on, hence ending up in the wrong hands of some men.

There are few similarities in regards to the men, but it is mostly women who end up in abuse. Men deal with their emotions too by drinking, smoking and also abusing substances, and a small percentage of men can also fall into the category of being promiscuous. It almost feels like it makes them feel good. In another words, it feels like a gap is being filled to solve a problem, but looking at it closely, that is not necessarily the case. Let's not forget too, that cheating and promiscuity is becoming very common these days amongst couples too.

Since they are still under the umbrella of "marriage", their bad habits tend to "slip under the rug". It is also very common for men to have many secret children outside while still legally married, and sleeping around is becoming very common for some married women. Like I mentioned earlier, both parties might have many so-called reasons for engaging in adultery. The amazing thing is, some still cast stones whilst they remain fully guilty and not having a single thought about changing their behaviour. For some, it feels like life as usual.

Another factor to consider is that for some women, having many sexual partners is actually a lifestyle that they might have naturally drawn towards. Some due to addiction and others just not bothered about it at all. Some also use it as a source of comfort to blank out life's issues. Some prefer it as an occupation. In the midst of it all, the sign of vulnerability is always seen in these kinds of situations.

Another common stigma is this; "most youths that are involved in crimes come from single parent homes". To some extent, I agree, but on the other hand, I think it's important to acknowledge the single parents whose children have successfully pulled through up to adulthood despite challenges. As our children grow up, they make decisions, some are right and some totally detrimental. This is mostly due to peer pressure, media pressure, so-called want-to-be celebrity pressure, to name a few. At present, it is looking like a fifty-fifty situation, as behaviour change in the lives of the youth has been caused by quite a few factors, so this is not only about single-parenting.

One major factor is the case where both parents are still present but due to horrible and sometimes exhausting work schedules, the children are left unsupervised for long periods of time. In some homes, the mother goes to work in the morning, then dad goes at night, and whenever each return back from work, it's mostly to go straight to sleep. Once a parent wakes up, there are chores to do and the trail continues. In this situation it is most likely that both parents have limited time for their children. Not only are they busy chasing money to look after the family, and also to finance other ventures and extra extended family responsibilities, but also have housework to do and other household chores. This can be daunting and therefore leads to tiredness and sometimes ill-health. This kind of setup also affects the marital relationship, which then affects the children. Working with young people gives me a lot of insight into the emotional and social aspects when it comes to behavioural change. A lot of our children leave home and go to school because by law they have to be in school. Parents should be shocked by the amount of children that are causing problems in school not because they want to, but because they are simply looking for attention, love and care though some children still have to deal with social issues around their peers. Self-harm was recently added to one of the signs to watch out for amongst our young people. Self-harm is one typical cry for emotional help. The majority of parents can say "oh well", we provide our children with everything they want, some even expensive technical gadgets and games, and also designer clothing. Extra tuition also paid for.

Basically, everything is provided and the child does not need to complain but just get on with their education. It all sounds good. Yes! Well done to every hard working family out there. Some parents have also managed this pattern of living and it has worked for them. This can also be successful due to the strong foundation that has been established. Also, this can be achieved based on the choices the child makes as they grow up. I am not saying this pattern of running one's home is completely out of order. Not at all! But also, let's not forget that life is holistic, and not just centralised. Our children need to be emotionally, socially and where possible spiritually fit too. There must be a balance. I must commend some families that have been well balanced in raising up their children, and I believe in giving praises where it is due. However, failure to ensure this balance is what leads some of our young people to the streets. Obviously, in addition to socially related challenges such as peer pressure and "get it quick mentality". We always ask the question; what are they finding on the streets? They have at least if not all things, something to keep them going. This then brings me back to the point of the child making certain decisions that the parents cannot override, especially living in a society where 100% human rights have been given to our children and with the interference of social services and child protection. It almost seems like a battle between parents and children, and then the government and parents. Some parents have completely lost the plot when it comes to running their homes. Obviously some are due to some of the things discussed above, but some because of the pressure of local government interference on how to or not to raise our children.

Again, we can say that is too much of a one-sided mentality to have. Just because a parent is called to order by children's services about the way they discipline their child, or sometimes a child is put into care as a result of physical abuse by a parent, it does not remove their complete right for the care of their remaining children. It certainly causes some self-esteem issues for some parents, who may have innocently and not necessarily meant to harm their child. Also, due to some of the accusations that some of our children make against us as parents, where it seems the side of the child is always taken even before hearing from the parent. So some parents just feel that their rights have been snatched off them. Some even scared to take any form of action regarding their children. Some feel their children are in control of their home. Some always worried about their child's school questioning the child about issues at home; all of these tend to add to the decline of healthy youth living.

There is therefore no binding evidence to say that it is only children from one parent homes that end up on the streets, or in trouble. So many other factors can be responsible in addition to what is mentioned above.

Yes! I fully agree that to some extent, that single parents take the hit for certain social declines, but I would encourage my readers to look more into this for themselves before giving the final verdict. Let's not forget to also take into consideration that government implemented laws regarding the rights of young people have not helped.

Giving the child leeway by saying to them when you are stressed by your parents, "you can leave their home and ask the council to re-house you", or sometimes encourage children to go into foster care for some minor issues that would have been resolved easily between parent and child. The child is separated and taken into care where there is mostly no binding relationship between carer and the child except for ensuring they are safe. A lot of families feel let down sometimes by social services. I am in no way condoning violence against a child and giving all the rights to the parent; not at all! There are definitely extreme cases that cannot be compromised on. What tends to happen is that our children are placed in hostels where they are now introduced to drugs and gangs, fraudulent activities,(the list goes on), ending up in jail or actually losing their lives. Yes, we can say they should have chosen rightly, but for goodness sake, they are still children and they need guidance as best as they can receive. Yes, government is trying to ensure our children are well protected, but providing a roof for the child is not the only solution to the child's life. Giving them money for their physical welfare and sending them to some counsellor doing their job just to "tick a box" has not proven any fruitful for our children. There is more to the situation, and it needs to be deeply reviewed by all entities involved. I sincerely respect the role of the social services and child protection in the communities. They definitely do their best. They are also guided by rules and guidelines. Parents and families do feel sometimes that there are some misjudgements in some situations.

Another factor for the social and behavioural decline in our youth is the fact that there are not many activities available to engage our children. Quite a lot of centres are closing due to cuts made by the government, thereby leaving our children exposed to grooming by so-called gang lords.

Recently, Channel 4 aired a documentary on how our youngsters were recruited into prostitution, drug running, and being forced to carry out various criminal activities. The youngsters are then promised a great future. Some are being provided with expensive designer clothing and electronic gadgets. In addition, the youngsters are encouraged to convince their peers to join their gang. They instil so much fear in them by brainwashing them about the horrible things that will happen if they pull out or escape. They tell them that they are not safe except when with them. One of the gang lords claimed that their targets were youngsters from single parent homes. This really petrified me, knowing that I am a single mother. I had to ensure my children watched the documentary. Since then, I have been reminding them daily about being content with what they have, not to take other people's property without their consent. And another important instruction; not talking to strangers, especially when asked personal questions. I try very hard to teach my children to walk in integrity, and I try to leave by example as much as I can. But sadly, on some occasions, they have not made some good choices. I had to call in other parties sometimes in order to have an apt mediation. One thing I have and am still learning to do is seek help or support where needed from trusted individuals. These can be role models or mentors both spiritual and secular. One can also seek support sometimes from other trusted family members and also from your child's peers living exemplary lives. There are many young people who mentor their peers and the results are mostly good too. We should never be ashamed of asking for support just because it will make us seem weak, or useless, or cause people to gossip about us. Seeking support also helps us to learn from one another. I am pretty sure most of us can relate to this. There is a very common saying that "It is a community that raises up a child". I used to really love this saying as it has worked for me on several instances. Sadly, this team spirit is fast fading away due to the following reasons;

Abuse is on the increase, and the statistics tell us that perpetrators are mostly people we know i.e., a family friend, or from a religious organisation. They can also be from the educational setting of a young person. What about those who have been instructed to protect our young People? It almost seems as if perpetrators are all hiding under the cover of their professions. This means there is no longer trust amongst families and other related bodies. As parents, we are constantly watching out for our children to the point of being paranoid. I have been like that many times. This might sound so bad, but that's just the way it is. Some families have gone overboard by over-protecting their children, some have withdrawn their children from mainstream educational settings, opting for home-schooling, with the hope they can place a tab on their children. Some of us might want to describe such as very extreme, but the point is that if parents feel they have been let down by all and sundry, they now tend to take what might be described as drastic actions. The question is; who can be trusted? This leads me to the second reason why community spirit is dwindling.

Many are scared of being accused falsely. They therefore put a boundary immediately between themselves and others in the community. Relationships are functioning but with no volume or impact. So many people have developed the "I don't care mentality" or live by the saying "I just mind my own business". Some adults can walk past a group of young people being anti-social in their neighbourhood or on the streets, but fail to correct them for fear of retribution, or false accusation. Some of us fail to testify against someone in court, as there is the fear of little or no protection at all. Recently, a very young life was terminated by a gang in the east end of London. It was claimed the deceased was a witness in court for a rape case which took place a few years ago. Such events can be of huge discouragement to responsible citizens, or even when someone is a victim. Some victims of crimes have also suffered in silence for failure to report acts of perpetrators due to fear of retribution. How sad can this be? What on earth is becoming of the society we live in?

The massive cut in funds by the government, to run activity centres has also pushed our communities to underperform. In time past, there used to be individuals in the community with various skills volunteering to run centres that will cater for our young people, keeping them off the streets, and engaging their minds with various activities. This was a big help for those parents who could not afford paid activities for their children.

At present, many of the youth centres are closed which has left a lot of our young people on the streets, also exposing them to crime. This closure also affects parents and toddler activities, which used to be very popular, as parents will also use that opportunity to bond with their children at a young age. I personally benefited from these activities fifteen years ago while my children were between the ages of 2-5. It also used to be a great avenue for parents to network and share ideas together. All of this really did help to maintain a healthy community.

At the moment, community morale is low, and this spreads right across the boroughs and cities in the UK. Also, many of those volunteers have no time these days to sacrifice as they need to work extra hours to support their cost and standard of living. I have just laid all of this here for us readers to see and try to grasp the bigger picture.

Another common stigma or stereotype is that single parents are lazy and prefer staying at home on benefits instead of working. In addition, they prefer having lots of children. They sometimes live in expensive accommodation. This is a big topic right here and I am going to try my best to analyse it.

The benefits system has been instituted for donkey years as a means of support to those who need it to a large extent, and also to majority of inhabitants but on a low scale depending on circumstances. It also means that at some point, one has to be means tested to be awarded benefits. Also, after reaching a certain threshold in one's income, they will no longer be eligible for benefits. The system can also be detrimental to the future of many claimants as it has a way of keeping people in, and if not careful can end up with a lot of people in poverty. People used to refer to benefits as "free money" in time past, some would say "it is government cash" so many people just went in for it as it almost seems as if it was very easy to get, even foreigners could come into the country and the next thing to do was to head down immediately to the benefit office or council.

The benefit system is no longer a safe haven for many, as it used to be. Even when qualified for certain forms of benefit, some claimants are being put through so much stress as they go through the process. Rigorous checks are made to allow claimants on the system. This is definitely as a result of the benefits system being abused. People claim all sorts of benefits such as income support, job seekers allowance, child benefit, incapacity/disability, maintenance, housing and council tax, carers, working and child tax benefits. Not to forget other goodies such as medical exemption certificates and subsidised prescriptions on the NHS. If we are to be honest with ourselves as we read this book, most of us might have claimed a certain type of benefit then and even now.

We also need not forget that claimants were not only single parents; some were an entire household, some just couples either together or separated still managed to claim benefits. Older people are also part of the claimant procedure. Yes! back in the days the system was abused, and despite rigorous actions being taken to tackle benefit fraud in this present age, it is still hard work for the bodies concerned. My question is: why label and demonise single parents only? After all, that is how it seems. The percentage of claimants from single parent led households might be slightly higher, but let's not ignore the fact that claims are made from other categories of individuals too.

What can we say about some claimants who fake their sickness and go to the extent of paying for a sickness note at their GP practice, just to go on incapacity benefit? What can we say about couples who make claims for benefits by claiming they are separated? For example the husband in one town and wife in another, all down to unaccountability of how much income they earn as a couple. In addition, we have heard stories of couples or families claiming housing benefits from one postcode to the other, obviously through fraudulent means. It makes one to wonder how on earth they had the guts to do that.

Some claimants have owned various properties whereby renting out and still receiving benefits without informing the government or council where possible.

We all should know by now how the National Health Service has began their effective charge for health services used by certain categories of people. In times past, all these were free. Many foreigners used to benefit from the NHS, ranging from free maternity services to registering at GP practices, and also for medical checkups. The rate of abuse of the system was high and with all it's hard work on clamping down, the UK government has struggled a bit in tackling this trend. Progress is been made slowly but surely. Attached is the link for all statistics compiled by the DWP (Department of work and pensions).It is very detailed, looks a bit complicated, but I believe it is good for us all to have some form of knowledge into these things.

DWP benefits statistics 2018 - GOV.UK

DWP *benefits statistics* 2018. *Statistics* on DWP administered *benefits*. Published 21 February 2018. Last updated 13 November 2018 — see all updates.

Above are just a few instances mentioned, and I want to believe that as we read on, some of us might have many more to add on if we were to re-write this book.

In the midst of all of this chaos, it saddens me that single parents are mostly stereotyped or singled out. I have to be honest with writing this book, and I encourage every reader to have a balanced perspective into this situation. It is always bigger than we think. I encourage us to assess situations first before making that final judgement. I had made this statement previously that "my thinking on single parents was very biased in the beginning", but being in a position of single parenting changed my thinking and perspective completely. Well! Thank God for that, as I now believe that each situation is always different, and things will be much better if only we assess and reassess these situations.

Yes, I agree that through the years, some single parents have abused the system. This can be down to certain individual mindsets also in relation to culture, tradition and religion.

If a woman is coming from a background where it is not a must to go out and fend for the family, then it is very easy for that person to stay home forever. Some cultures believe that the place for women is in the home (women are homemakers), where they are responsible for looking after children and looking after their husbands, satisfying them on every angle, cooking, washing, school runs and the list goes on.

Even though we now live in the working and technological age, and where society has open up some form of female emancipation, there are yet still many women who don't find anything wrong staying at home. Let's not forget also that looking after the home is a round the clock job. Some women actually like it, while you have some who want some kind of balance, preferring to work part-time or even full time.

There are some women who feel great that they can actually stay home while hubby goes out to fend. It is a man's thing and they do take pride for it. Should we now frown on these women because of their choice? This is a question for all to deal with. The reality is, not every woman whether married or single will go out there to work. Some families are financially well off, and need no help from the government. Some might have gained their wealth through building up of successful business, some through family inheritance, also some by walking in high paid jobs, some have their spouses retiring with big payouts or bonuses. Naturally, for some women from such affluent background, they would prefer staying at home and ensuring quality healthy life for their family. They are proud to call themselves "housewives". Some are notorious for big spending, buying expensive top range cars, designer wears and going on exclusive holidays. The question is why not frown at such categories of women? They are wives and they believe they deserve to be number one partakers of their husband's earnings. To be honest who will not want to have and enjoy a comfortable lifestyle?

I re-emphasize again, that we should not be quick to stereotype. Not all single parents want to live permanently on the dole (benefits). The majority of single parents have actually thought about working, or even tried working but failed to continue for several reasons.

I did mention previously about some kinds of mindsets that some might have. Some mindsets can be positive but some completely negative and not beneficial in the long term. A single parent mother or father might have given up on life, and all they can fathom for themselves is "there is no other way out" so i am just going to stay on benefit. Some say things like "at least it is better than nothing". This can be due to the fact that some parents are actually depressed, some going through mental issues and children in care, some on drugs and alcohol and in and out of rehabilitation. The government has no option but to continue to provide for their welfare as it is against the law and for human rights purposes.

There is also job seeker allowance which pays a weekly some to those people looking for job with proof that they are actually looking. People are sometimes threatened that their support will stop if effort is not made. Some people actually do succeed in getting jobs, but in the end will dropout. This might be because they just cannot cope with working and are used to getting free taxpayers' money. Also this might sound funny and judgemental, but some people have a phobia for working. I can also say that the systems in place seem to be of help, but at the same time, prove detrimental to many. For example, in the United Kingdom, the Jobcentre normally expects individuals to record the number of job searches made including telephone numbers of those organisations. There were criteria for every claimant on Job Seekers Allowance (or job seeking part of what is now called Universal Credit). A claimant should have made at least ten job searches before their next appointment at the Jobcentre. It is normally every two weeks, for some every week based on circumstances. Failure to adhere to the job search rules will end up in the claimant getting their allowance suspended.

I can vividly remember what I went through as a job seeker. I had a booklet they used to give me in those days to log my searching activities, and trying to fill it in was very frustrating. It was not just about filling it in, but ensuring I phoned the places where I was looking for vacancies before logging it in the book. I used to be scared that perhaps they would call to find out whether I was saying the truth.

Honestly, because I was desperate, I tried very hard to go by the book in the first few weeks of my job search. But as time went on, the logging was like an exercise, sometimes I did fill it in properly and other times would just not bother. Not that I wasn't serious but it was not producing any fruit for me, especially due to the kind of jobs I was looking for.

Fortunately, I got a job just two months into my claim, and I was very happy to inform the case worker immediately. In addition, I felt so free that I did not have to update the booklet anymore. It felt like a burden on my shoulders. The booklet works for some in a sense that it pushes one to go out there and search for a job, and some people do make the effort to do that. However, to others, it's just like daily exercise. Some people like doing it for months and months and would prefer lying about their job searches just to fill in the log book, so that they continue getting their allowance. This is not limited just to single parents but to any other job seeking claimant. This is another area that is mostly abused, and it can be by anyone, and again not only by single parents.

Employers' unwillingness to offer flexible working hours to parents can also be a very big hindrance to employment. On one hand the government wants parents to work but on the other hand, nothing has been done to highlight the benefits of this to employers. It is not encouraging at all and therefore puts parents off. The next thing is to give up completely which then sends them back to claiming "job seeker allowance" I do understand that offering flexible or lesser contracts can seem like an obstacle for employers. However, it would be great to have a balance. It is not a must for everyone to work full time, let's face the fact. We must respect parents' choice of working hours. Some choose to work full time and others part-time. It is quite unfair to penalize parents or judge them for making choices that do not favour employers. But let me remind us once again about one of the stereotypes I mentioned earlier; the decline in the behaviour of our youths. One of the main factors is because none of the parents are at home as they are out earning money for the family. Also due to the fact that the government is trying hard to push as many as they can into work. Finding that balance can be challenging, trying to be flexible with parents and at the same time harsh.

I work full time as a single parent, and I know what it takes and how it feels to do this as well as grocery shopping, cooking, laundry, cleaning, monitoring children, creating and spending time with them, looking after all other bills and the list goes on. Oh wow! All glory and praise be to my Father. I can boldly testify that it has definitely not been by might nor by my own power, but by His Spirit indeed. His grace has brought me this far as I do really wonder how I have travelled such a distance. As we read this, I believe many of you can relate to this.

I know what it takes to create time to speak to my daughter after I have come back from work, just to give her my ears, though I really struggle to sometimes. She makes me laugh as failure to give her audience will lead her to complaining "Mum! You never listen when I speak". I must confess that I actually don't on a few occasions; simply because I am tired once I arrive home and just want to chill out a bit even before having my meal.

However, our children want us. They can be self-centred but we cannot blame them. That is the stage they are at for now where they need our attention, and we have to give it to them.

In terms of cutting down on my hours, I still look forward to the time I will be able to do so. In as much as I can work full time, it does not qualify me to judge others for not working full time. Quite a lot of parents, especially mothers, are best known for resigning from their jobs as they cannot get flexible contracts. Some parents prefer to transfer to agencies that send them to different places to work. It simply means parents like these are able to have some control of their own time. They decide to work only certain days in the week. Some parents might end up applying for a top up (working tax credits) as long as they have not hit a certain threshold in their finances. Some parents do decide to take a complete break by staying home until their children are a bit older.

The trend of fathers taking paternity or shared leave is also becoming popular as they are beginning to realize that their presence in the lives of their children as they develop is very important. Quite a few fathers are actually reducing their hours to stay home on a long term basis. Such a trend was not popular some few years ago. Also quite a lot of parents these days are going through so much stress due to the fact that they have to leave their children in nursery for between eight to ten hours every day just to go to work. Some parents feel so much guilt that they are not in their children's lives especially during their early stages. It is also showing that some parents are not all about the money, even though it is a key element, but also about that physical and emotional care provided for their children. These are men and women with a complete family unit; in fact a lot of what is being stated here has less to do with single parents only. Childcare and work related issues affect the majority of parents as a whole.

The financial element of childcare has also contributed to parents' decisions to either stay home completely, or stay in work but on reduced hours. It almost feels as if all we do as parents is to spend all our money on childcare. It is expensive and many cannot afford it these days despite being subsidized by the government. Some parents have resorted to having Au Pairs flown into the country to look after their children. It is quite cheaper to pay Au Pairs than giving all their money to a private nursery.

It is also advantageous for the children as they would be at home instead of being cared for outside. Some families are also supported by their family members and sometimes friends. Let us also not forget that some parents do not have recourse to public funds based on the type of residence permit they have in the country.

I am close to some families who are currently struggling with childcare. Some are high end professionals and some normal hardworking families who want to work and live a decent family life, but childcare is a major hindrance. I experienced this for a period of time when I started working many years ago. I must say a very big thank you to my loved ones who helped me with babysitting the children whenever they could. I had to work with agencies to enable me to manage my own schedule, as I could not work on a permanent basis. But as time went by and as they were growing up, I started readjusting my work too. Their school times were favouring me which means I did not have to pay childcare as I was able to pick them up from school, then we all got home together. Fortunately for me, there were days when I could leave my children in the after school club for a very reasonable fee. I also remember that while I was doing this juggling in between work and childcare, there were some people I knew in my neighbourhood who would normally ask me questions such as "why are you punishing yourself?" meaning I should stay home until my children were a bit bigger. I would respond by saying "no it was fine" and that I could manage.

These were mostly women in their fifties to sixties (flashback to what was stated about mindset).

On the other hand, I also encountered women my age who would gossip about me not working, even though they knew nothing about my life. And I used to think to myself, what if that was really the case? Why did they judge me even without checking to see what was happening? Not that some were available to help with childcare, but it was just easy to talk and cast blame on me. This is what often happens in society (the blame game).

As I write this book, my thoughts on these matters continues to broaden. I did mention previously how going through this process of single parenting has helped broaden my perspective on quite a lot of things.

So what am I saying? Yes! There are some loopholes. Some single parents whether male or female, have fallen way below and have not met expectations. Yes! Some have failed woefully and to some extent we can see how this is affecting our communities and society as a whole. I urge us all to remember that this can be down to several reasons. On the other hand, there are many who are steady-headed and trying their best by working hard to ensure the best for their children.

As I draw the curtain on this topic of stereotypes and stigma, I encourage us all to have a rethink, and also try to have at least some form of understanding on situations before tagging someone along. Things get much better when situations are viewed and assessed holistically not necessarily on an individual basis. We have got to look at the bigger picture.

CHAPTER 4

Celebrating Achievements

I titled it this way as I feel that due to the negative attention that single parents get, there is not much recognition or acknowledgement of the achievements of single parents and their families.

Despite challenges in life as single parents, I have discovered that being a single parent is not a barrier to achieving. Yes! it does mean an extra push and some strong determination, but again naturally in life, everyone goes through phases, people choose to move on and not allow life's challenges to get in their way. Hindrances do not apply to only single parents but to everyone both young and old. Achievements can come in various ways. For a single parent to raise their child or children amidst all the struggles, and for that child or those children to get through education, university or vocational career path, get a job, marry and have their own family, being a responsible citizen or impacting positively on the lives of other people can be seen as a great achievement. This is what a normal family expects anyways. However, if the family of a single parent achieves at least some of that, it might still be deemed as a big achievement. As mentioned earlier, achievements can be gained in several ways not necessarily in the above order.

I believe it is fair to start with my own story just to encourage someone out there that you can achieve something as long as you push for it and continue to persevere.

I have been widowed for ten years now with my two children, a boy 16 and a girl soon to be 14. For me, my first achievement will be, just being able to bring my children up to this stage. My son is preparing for his post 16 education, and my daughter preparing for her GCSEs. Wow! For me that's an achievement, as I never thought I would cope with raising them on my own. It has been very challenging in the present climate that we are living in. So by the help of God and all parties involved, we have managed to get to this stage. I really want to thank God. This might look like nothing to some people, but I cannot afford to take this for granted. I am so thankful for this. Yes! I went through some periods of stress here and there, just getting through to maintain the bills in the house, ensuring the children are happy and not feeling left out, managing and being content with the little we have, to remain in sound mind, not losing my children to social services and many more. For me, it's a win by his grace only. O wow! For every single dad and mum who has seen their children through their education, I say "well done", "kudos" to you all. If you are reading this and still feel like you have not achieved this, then my advice and encouragement will be to keep pushing and not give up. You shall surely get there.

By the special grace of the Father, and with the help from all my leaders, teachers, mentors, and encouragers through the years, I am also celebrating my existence in serving actively in the ministry of the body of Christ for fifteen years. Five years prior to this was dedicated to raising my children which made me a little inactive but still committed to the household of faith. I am currently serving as an assistant Pastor in my local assembly, and it has been a privilege and pleasure to serve others. I would be deceiving myself and you all reading this if I say the road leading to this has been smooth.

Not at all! I always wonder and ask myself as to how I got here. The first answer is yet again the grace, and secondly determination and perseverance plus the willingness to develop those gifts that are inside of me. I had to make up my mind that I will not allow my status to define me or make me feel inferior in any way, shape or form. I am in no way perfect but improving on myself daily to get to that point, as that is God's desire for us to be perfected. Through faith and courage, I started using my story to encourage others and also minister to people where necessary. I decided to reach people instead of going into a withdrawal syndrome which tends to happen when we find ourselves in certain situations. As I mingled with people and invested my time with whatever little I had to share with others through the years, it helped me greatly to heal up and also with moving forward.

I thank the Lord also for His grace to focus daily and also to be accountable to others who would normally check on me on a daily basis just to ensure I was on track. Yes indeed! There were (and still are) many distractions which would have diverted me from such a good cause, but I cannot thank my Lord enough! I am also very grateful for Him connecting me with like-minded people who carried my burden upon their shoulders to ensure I am where I am today. Therefore, I see this as a big achievement.

I encourage you all to start reflecting on those areas in your lives that you might have overlooked or just taken for granted just because it did not look tangible; remember what I said earlier on; that some achievements can be visible and some not. Why not celebrate yourselves for both?

Despite the ups and downs in life, and by the grace and strength of the lord, I have managed to maintain my job on a full time basis, which is not easy, but still I'm still pulling through. I know exactly what I mean, but it takes someone else to be in my shoes to be able to understand what and how it feels.

Another thing I am grateful for is to be able to maintain my home, striving very hard to ensure the rent and other bills are paid. Quite a lot of people have lost their homes and are in temporary accommodation or sofa surfing or street homeless for various reasons. It could have been myself in that same position. It just takes one crisis to hit one and this can affect every area in our lives. I have seen and spoken to many homeless people on different occasions, and in previous times when we have done some outreach in collaboration with another local church in my borough. I hear their stories; some do testify of some of the mistakes they made but some just found themselves in a series of unfortunate situations which landed them in that position of homelessness. Therefore, for me to have a roof over my head, I am grateful. This might sound funny, but I used to watch TV programs about bailiffs coming to repossess people's homes and other possessions, and I would pray so hard not to find myself in that situation, warning my children constantly on how we must manage with what we have, and not to go overboard as it can be very easy to find ourselves in such positions if we ignore even the simple things. I can go on and on with a few more, but for me, I can say these are the most important for me. I am grateful!

Secondly, I would like to celebrate all the single mums and dads who work in various professions and vocations. I have met countless individuals firstly in my place of work, some teachers, others heads of departments, nursery nurses and assistants, teaching assistants; all these positions held by either a single parent mum or dad. Lest I forget, there are also lots of principals, head teachers, vice and deputies. I have seen science technicians, food technicians and lots more. These are all in the education industry, and these positions are equally held by individuals who are married too. I am also celebrating single mums and dads working in the medical industry, from doctors to nurses and many more positions in that field. I can testify to this as I personally have quite a lot of family members and also friends and associates in this industry. Salutations to those working in council departments, the social services, the police, the army, banking, law, civil service and other vocational professions such as sports, mentoring and coaching, beauty and many more. I also celebrate those working in the religious organisations. We have reverends, pastors, vicars, evangelists, priests, teachers, apostles, prophets, leaders, imams, and lots more.

I also want to celebrate my single parents in business. Quite a lot of them operating excellently in this area of gifting, and are totally committed to it. I learnt to celebrate the various gifts in the lives of people and to respect whatever career path they choose to follow as long as they are functioning well in it. Even if there are challenges, people do not quit but continue to persevere. Through the years, I have also seen some hard working single ladies leading successful charitable organisations, some of which I have personally supported. Their drive and passion is extraordinary. I have highlighted the above and most of what is here is what I have seen around. In all of these careers and vocations, regardless of location, one is likely to find out that single parents do occupy these positions.

I mentioned earlier that being single is just a status and should not be a hindrance to one's progress though those hindrances show up every now and then. But this is part of life. We fall down and we are not supposed to stay there but get back up and continue to strive. I do realise some individuals struggle with this, but at the same time let's not take our eyes off the positive things going on around us.

I remember my years of growing up in Africa, where you find parents who are not educated nor attained any form of success, but are also very keen to see their children succeed in life. How does that sound? This might sound weird but yes it is quite true. Comparing the standard of life in Africa to that in Europe is quite a big margin, and sadly with the vast array of opportunities available in Europe, there are still some families who never take advantage of such of them. But then again, as mentioned earlier, some of the reasons might still have to do with mindset. The irony though is that even for those families who thought that they have failed in life, they still try their best to encourage their children to achieve well enough for their future. Most parents do not want their children to make the same mistakes they did in their past, and for this reason encourage or even push their children very hard. Some actually put quite a lot of pressure on their children. I am going to be honest to say that on quite a few occasions, I have pushed my children a bit harder just because I want to over-protect them, and wanting the best for them especially due to the fact that I am still working hard though a bit limited sometimes. But our children are surrounded by such a cloud of opportunities that they cannot afford to miss out. I know they can go to places if they put in just a little more effort.

On this note, I celebrate every single mother or father who has walked past their weaknesses, challenges and failures just to support their children to the best of their abilities. As we all read this and take our minds back just a little bit, we can all recall some parents in our family circle, amongst our friends, our neighbourhoods who have or are still going through hardship but working hard just to ensure the future of their child or children is bright, obviously with the child's cooperation, as the children also have a role to play to ensure their success.

Barack Obama, former president of the United States of America was actually brought up by his single mother. I also read about quite a number of celebrities right across industries who were brought up by a single parent. These people have worked hard and have become very successful. In this same manner, I acknowledge every one of you reading this, if you were brought up by a single parent and have worked hard to get you to where you are in life. We have a great deal of successful people in our societies who were brought up by single parents. Sadly, it doesn't appear that such successful single parenting is documented or counted.

Finally, I also want to acknowledge single parent dads and mums whose full time commitment is to stay at home. Staying at home is a full time job on its own, and those who practice it well surely receive the harvest for it. We need to realise that everyone has what they are called to do and become, and as a society we must accept and respect those parents that choose to stay at home instead of chastising them. It is their choice, and some have been graced with it, meaning the ability to do it that way. Some of us want may be a little balance between work and home. That is fine too. Let's not forget that the dynamics of every family is different.

One more time, I say kudos to all you single parents out there. Keep pushing and do not give up. If you feel you are failing, or being pressured and perceived wrongly, my advice is to do your best and leave the rest, for time will surely tell. As I have encouraged you, continue to be your own cheerleader.

Remember! Being single is just a status, and for some it might change after a while, but for some not. However, whether it changes or not, as a single parent, we can all still be successful.

Below is an extract found on "raisingchildren.net.au" which is an Australian parenting website. It reads as follows;

> *"**Single** parenting and **successful** families. Here's the good news: **children raised** by **single parents** are generally just as happy as **children** living with two biological **parents**. ... Whether you're a*

***single parent** or partnered, if you spend time with your **child**, he's more likely to be happy and mentally healthy."*

CHAPTER 5

Lessons and Tips for Single Parents

Throughout my single parent journey, I have personally learnt a lot in terms of what to do and not do. We always use statements like "experience is the best teacher", meaning one can only learn and become a better person after going through things in life. These are the things I have learnt from my personal experiences so far and just from observing the trend in general. We can learn from each other's experiences too. I believe this might encourage someone reading this in case you find yourself in a similar position. Some of these lessons and tips can also be applied in other areas of life and whether you're single or not. Therefore, I believe it can encourage us all. In addition, I cannot stress enough how important it is for us to take a review of our lives every now and then, to see what has gone well so far, and also what should be or not be taken further; or even better if. Failure to do so will end us in the same cycle over and over again.

Lesson 1

The first lesson I have learnt in this journey is not to rush into relationships here and there hoping it is a final solution to one's singleness. This pattern has not been successful for the majority of people. I sometimes feel that due to pressure coming from society, and due to the emotional gap in people's lives, individuals feel the need to enter into relationship as soon as possible, once the other is done with. Remember, I mentioned in the beginning of this book that singleness can be caused in various ways. Using myself as an example, I got to this point because of the loss of my husband. I could remember the several phone calls I had from various men who thought they would just warm their way into my life and home easily.

The first thing was, that I felt extremely vulnerable; like all of a sudden I was uncovered or exposed, or had no one to cover my back. I'm just been honest.

Secondly, for me that would have just been a misplaced priority. I didn't even know how to start mourning the loss of my husband, next thing was looking at our two beautiful children and wondering how they were going to survive with me only, how I was going to survive financially and the questions of 'how' kept going on and on. My emotions were just all over the place, and thoughts of surviving the present and the future were my focus. I felt so wounded and deeply hurt and did not know when I could come out.

We can all see the amount of baggage I was carrying personally. Yes, I had people around me who supported me and this was on a regular basis, phone calls and the lot, but I needed time to get acquainted to my new status or circumstance. There was no quick fix to the situation. This was a matter of time and process. I realised I could not fast-forward my life at that point nor go for quick fixes which we tend to do most of the time and end up with more problems. What about my children? They were vulnerable too. How could I introduce them to someone that quickly? What would they have thought about me? That I was desperate or what? Did I care about their own emotions too? Would they have been ready for that yet? If I had gone ahead into a relationship, did I find the time to vet the man, as to his past and present? Whether married, divorced, separated or in a similar position to mine? What baggage would the man or woman have? Would they come in just to make the most of the opportunity and for their own selfish reasons only? All of these things deserve consideration before venturing.

One might argue that it is sometimes difficult to figure someone's secrets, but there is no smoke without fire. One is definitely bound to find out some truths if very observant, no matter the secret of the person coming into our lives. The problem is we tend to turn a blind eye and very quickly make such decisions. We go into it hoping "oh well, it will be good".

For my case I learnt it would not have been fair even for the man coming into our lives as our wound of loss was yet very raw. The man coming into our lives would be happy and hopeful that things are going to work out for him too. But because we as a family had not gone through our healing process properly, it would lead to a lot of issues that would send the relationship into disarray. Yes, some relationships might be too quick and yet still with very genuine intentions, and truly some do get on straight away. But the success rate is very low. Based on my experience and observation of human behaviour, process and time are very important. There is no need to rush, and we always use statements like "what is for us will never run ahead of us", meaning we will surely get it regardless of hindrances or obstacles, whilst doing what is needed to get it. I learnt that one of the things we must realise is to avoid taking some very important actions when we are vulnerable, or actually first of all identify that we are vulnerable. Our failure to recognise this means we will be opening ourselves to emotional and physical abuse which can be so detrimental and in the end cause some long term damage.

This is a case that was very dear to me. The whole saga started a few years ago with a couple who have both passed away now leaving two beautiful children between themselves and another five between the late husband and previous relationships. This is just one example as I know there are many others with a little variance.

As we read on, we will see and try to understand and align our viewpoints too. This was in the case of death. I also want to reiterate that this is not a judgement in any shape of form, but I believe we can all relate to this.

As mentioned earlier, this couple had two beautiful children and it looked like everything was going well, until death knocked on the beautiful life of the wife due to a very brief illness. This came as a shock to everyone. It knocked me even further as she passed on my birthday. She passed on and no sooner, her husband started murmuring during his interactions with people that he was going to find someone as he could not stay on his own. He actually gave himself six months to find a woman. Prior to the six-month deadline, a particular lady was always visiting the house, whom he introduced as a family friend. As time went by this lady friend was being seen at the premise almost every day. This became a regular routine and by the time it was six months, the lady friend was already pregnant. It looked like she was about five to six months gone already. Everyone was filled with awe. They were both adults, and knew exactly what they were doing. A question that popped up was; were they seeing each other prior to him losing his wife? Hmmm! This process was just too quick and everyone around could feel the vibe of anger from the wife's family and also for the poor children involved. They had no choice but to just get on with the flow. One might think that the first thing on the woman's agenda would be to pay attention to the children's emotional needs, show them she was there for them, comfort and encourage them. Not at all! Indeed, she had her own agenda. The lady had her first son and soon after that she had a second one, obviously making the most of the opportunity to have children as she never had children before. For her, that was beneficial, but this also contributed to her lack of attention and care for the other two. Her two boys were her focus and everyone around them could see that the other two were not well tended to. A clash of culture was also a big issue in this case. There was a big strain on the relationship between the new wife and children. More so, they were young people and it generally takes them a while to get accustomed to someone else in general.

Moving on, the new wife moved out of the husband's house together with her two boys and back to her flat on the other side of the city. There were visible signs of strain as it meant that caring for the other two would rest solely on their father. At the same time, the father had to travel across London to spend some time with his two younger boys. He was simultaneously running two homes. It was evident that things were not easy for this father despite him working very hard to please his family. Unfortunately, his life was cut short eight years after the death of his previous wife. The sad part to it was he died in the process of looking after his two homes. He had finished working on a Thursday night, passed by his two older children to leave some lunch money for the morning. They were definitely sleeping so they never got the opportunity to see him on that day. He then made his way to look after the two younger boys as their mum (his new wife) was travelling to her home country in Europe. It was claimed that he got to her flat late that night, sat down for a little chat and they both fell asleep on a sofa bed that was in the living room. The wife claimed that a very big sound was heard like someone having a very deep and long grunt. She was semi-conscious and the noise woke her up immediately. She jumped up and switched the lights on to see what was going on. She checked on him but he was not responding. She tried to do first-aid but to no avail. She then called the ambulance who showed up immediately, they tried too but they were unable to resuscitate him. He was taken to the hospital and put on life support and two days later his life support was turned off. The diagnosis was heart failure due to an aneurysm. It is a condition where the blood vessels in the brain are burst and causes haemorrhaging.

Apparently, there are quite a few other factors responsible for this condition, and the most common is high blood pressure of which can occur through genetics or generally due to other forms of stress to the body, and also bad eating habits and lifestyles. He did not show any of these symptoms except it was claimed that he took tablets for headaches. Also, no one knows whether he was going through stress due to running two homes.

Stress is another issue that is common with everyone, but again, a lot of men are normally shy to talk about it, being men with all pride and prestige. It is mostly likely he had high blood pressure too but maybe it was never checked it out. No one can attest to this. Now this is common mostly with men, as men generally do not like going to the hospital. Please be aware that this condition can be sudden too. It does not necessarily pick and choose as to who might have it.

Another way to put this is maybe that was just his time as things do happen when it is someone's time. There may be many schools of thought. My main focus is on the children who are left to go through the emotional torture. The older children are complete orphans now being looked after by a relative, and the younger ones still have their mum at least. I just could not fathom what the older children were and still going through. They were the same age with my two children. The eldest son managed to finish his secondary education and moved on to college then was planning to specialise in a sports related career. His sister is about to finish her secondary education too. I also feel for the younger ones too who have lost their dad, and also lost all contact with their step siblings through no fault of theirs, but due to the fact that dad's family decided to refuse contact between the new wife and the older children; which has not helped matters. To a point, I can understand their hurt too and the reasons for them being adamant. What about the new wife? As I mentioned earlier, she must have come in with the hope of having a perfect new family, but unfortunately for her the unforeseen events of life unfolded. She has to go through mourning, and possibly the guilt of not being there fully for those children, and also the fear of entertaining a new relationship. The ball is now in her court whether to give herself some time to heal and recover, and also to reassess individuals very well before making decisions to carry on into a relationship especially now that she has children too. It is definitely worth considering.

This case is one extreme example and the other person is unable to complete the story. He could have still been alive and based on the evidence of events so far, one can predict the future of that relationship already, since the wife had already moved out anyway.

We can also look at other scenarios such as someone coming out of separation, divorce or a violent relationship and entering another immediately without time to reflect, re-examine the how, what, why, what next etc. Some people do have different opinions when it comes to this, such as everything is a risk and people just have to try their luck. Yes I do agree to some extent, but we must also look at the negative side of entering from one relationship to the other. Some of us are so vulnerable that we easily end up in the hands of manipulators and wreckers, the very ones we trusted will do us harm.

Yes! Some relationships have been successful but most a shamble. It actually leaves some people extremely emotionally and sometimes physically damaged than before. Sadly, the children involved suffer too. Just think about it for a second; how is it possible for a parent to introduce their child or children to a number of men or women as their new dads or mums. Sometimes the children get confused too, and because they cannot voice it out, they suffer deep inside. This kind of pattern has also resulted in the large amount of rape, sexual and physical assault in families. I cannot imagine bringing a man into my home to first of all sleep with me, and also move on to sleep with my daughter or molesting my son or vice versa. Also, if they have other secret lifestyles such as drug and substance abuse, they are likely to indoctrinate my children. I have known quite a lot of people with such stories, some ended up losing their children to social services. Some of the things mentioned might be classified as extreme and we never get to consider the wellness of our children. It is very important we consider such as matters with high priority when making relationship decisions. We just cannot afford to ignore the very things that might come back to haunt us.

My decision of staying single up to the time of writing this book is due to the fact that I wanted my children to heal up and be stable. I have also been very weary of someone coming into our lives with wrong motives. I do believe and want the right candidate for myself and my children. If it means waiting a little bit longer, then so be it. I wait with joy. I just cannot afford to risk it. Has it been easy? Not at all! I can boldly say that! But the wait is worth it. I have peace of mind and I am trying to be content and disciplined too.

Some of us have various reasons for flowing with such patterns. Some people say they cannot afford to live without sex, or they just cannot cope with living by themselves. Yes! As good as sex can be for us, we cannot allow it to control us. At some point, we must learn to exercise some discipline. We are most likely to have sex with the wrong people when we are vulnerable. Some people have come into our lives just to satisfy our sexual needs and nothing more. Is that all to a relationship? Do we take into consideration the other roles that the man or woman can possibly play in our lives? Or are we just giving ourselves away so cheaply without any value placed on ourselves? Do we compromise so easily just so that we have someone in our lives? Or are we just trying to keep up with others? Wanting to have a partner is not a crime; it is actually good to have a great companion. However, ending up with the wrong one can have severe consequences. What happens next after falling out with that individual? Look for another sexual partner? I believe it is fair enough to respect someone's desire as to how they want to live their lives. But as parents, we should consider how taking such actions can have an adverse effect on our children. Sadly, some children can be the exact copy of their parents in terms of behaviour.

There is a popular statement we make "like father like son", or "like mother like daughter" and vice versa. Simply put; the things we do live after us if care is not taken.

In as much as our children might be lacking a father or mother figure in their lives, it is still best to take things one at a time instead of rushing. The good news is that it pays to wait patiently for something.

Lesson 2

Another lesson I have learnt during this journey is learning to manage my finances. As a single parent, this is key, knowing that you are the only physical source of provision for your family. It also means one has to prioritise as to what, how, when and where to spend money. Sometimes when it comes to shopping, I discovered that I bought things that I really did not need, either for myself or for the children. Also, when it comes to buying for our children, we need to be mindful of this; not buying things for them as a comfort or because their friends have got it.

If this pattern of fulfilling wants and not needs continues, one will be trapped for a long time. We must not forget that bills are supposed to be at the top of our list. I did mention earlier on about priorities. Making that list of what is important from highest to lowest is also very key. It's amazing how some of us parents prioritise. Someone sat with me some time ago to help me with my budgeting. She asked me about what my priorities were. I made my list in order as I deemed fit. She calmly told me, "I think you need to have a second look to see if you can rearrange your list again." Deep inside I was fuming as to who she was to tell me to reorder my priorities. In the end, I came to realise that she was actually right. I had to look at things from another angle. I believe a lot of us do struggle like I did when it comes to budgeting. Knowing our incomings and outgoings with regards to bills and other miscellaneous items is key.

I learnt that my outgoings should not supersede my income, which tends to happen with most of us if we can be honest with ourselves. Sometimes it is through no fault of ours, but things happen such as unforeseen events which most of us never plan for, or put something aside for. However, we have to try our best to protect this. The income can be in the form of a salary, or cash from other avenues such as business, and also benefits, and sometimes gifts from others. Outgoings can range from rent, council tax, insurance, road tax, water rates, gas and electricity, groceries, TV licence, internet and phone bills, clothes shopping, savings, eating out, extra family or charity funds, car servicing, fuel, birthdays and weddings or other celebrations, holidays, days out and funerals. Some outgoings can be weekly, monthly, quarterly or yearly. We can clearly see how long the list is, and maybe there are still some more things that needs to be added to the list depending on individual wants. Our lists can be as long as our wants. Wow!

I do realise that many single parents struggle on a day to day basis with most of the things on the above list if not all. This can be due to the fact that some might be on benefits, or in and out of jobs which causes problems, and for various reasons that cannot be unjustly judged. I have been there before so this is said out of experience. The benefits system can disrupt families so badly despite being there as a source of support.

However, it is going to take great discipline to manage our outgoings. Failure to manage our outgoings will eventually land us in huge financial problems.

Another issue that looms around as we talk about incomings and outgoings is that of "debt". I discovered an article online by Miles Brignall as I researched into this issue of debt. What I came across was scary. It reads as follows:

> [2]*"More than 6 million Britons don't believe they will ever be debt free, according to new research which has also found the average person in the UK owes £8,000 – on top of any mortgage debt. Almost a quarter of all Britons said they are struggling to make ends meet, while 62% said they were often worried about their levels of personal debt, according to research for Comparethemarket.com. Earlier this month, the price comparison website asked 2,000 adults detailed questions about their personal finances. They found that 10% of respondents had "maxed out" on a credit card, while a similar number said they had been overdrawn within the past 12 months. A third of those*

_____

[2]
https://www.theguardian.com/money/2017/oct/30/average-uk-debt-at-8000-per-person-not-including-the-mortgage

interviewed told researchers that they were already planning on taking on additional debt in the form of credit cards, loans car finance and mortgages in the next year. Over a third said they could not see themselves ever being in a financial position to help younger family members, breaking the tradition of the "bank of mum and dad". The results chime with a recent study by the Financial Conduct Authority which found that that 4.1 million people are already in serious financial difficulty. The survey, the biggest ever by the city regulator, concluded that half of the UK population are financially vulnerable, with 25- to 34-year-olds the most over-indebted. Shakila Hashmi, head of money at Comparethemarket.com, said: "Right now millions of Brits could be in danger of suffering from one of the longest financial hangovers in history. While it may be hard to see an end in sight, the worst thing people in debt can do right now is stick their head in the sand. As well as reining in spending, there are other ways you can reduce debt, like switching to credit cards that help you get on top of debt with interest-free periods." Hashmi said for those with credit card woes out of control, charities such as StepChange offer free and impartial advice to help get debt under control. Comparethemarket.com has created a new "debt free face" calculator, in which users input their personal finances and can upload a photo of themselves to learn how old they will be when they are debt-free (and what they will probably look like when that time comes). Last week the ratings agency Standard & Poor's warned that the rapid rise in UK consumer debt to £200bn is unsustainable and should raise "red flags" for the major lenders."

When it comes to borrowing money, I discovered that the system is created in a way that people are often encouraged to take credit despite their financial challenges. Checks are not done properly or at all, and money is offered to people at high interest rates which can take years to repay. I have had my own fair share of this, and by the grace of God, and with extreme actions put in place, I will be free very soon.

How many of us can attest to the fact that you have peace of mind when you are debt free? Absolutely free of major stress. Yes! There are always matters arising, but just imagine sorting out those matters and your debt at the same time; it is not a funny at all.

Coming out of debt might take a lot of effort, by phoning appropriate authorities or companies, arranging payment terms and conditions, trying to meet up with minimum, maximum or bulk payments, as the more money is paid, the earlier the debt is cleared. This can work based on individual circumstances at a particular time, but this can be feasible even if it means just doing the little that we can until it is all cleared.

Another great benefit of this would be to cut down completely on some lifestyle choices, which can help to put aside the extras needed. One cannot afford to live life as usual to attain debt clearance. This can only happen for a few. It can be painful, but knowing that it would just be for a period of time, and the opportunities given to also learn from this experience so that one will not find themselves in such a situation ever again.

There is a common saying that "experience is a teacher". Leaving or ignoring unpaid debts can come back to haunt people years down the line except for a few individuals who have had their debts completely written off. Some have also had a way of telling 'diplomatic' lies; hmm! And with a deep breath too, I managed to escape by giving some reasons so that their debt can be written off. I know paying off debts is last on some people's list for sure! But let's remember also that it is money that does not belong to us. Therefore, for morality and integrity sake, it is worth considering. There is a popular golden rule in the scriptures according to **Romans 13** that says; *" we should owe no one anything but only in love."*

Satisfaction and contentment is also very key as the following scriptures state;

> *"Keep your life free from love of money, and be content with what you have, for he has said, "I will never leave you nor forsake you".* **Hebrews 13:5**

> *"Not that I am speaking of being in need, for I have learned in whatever situation I am to be content. I know how to be brought*

*low, and I know how to abound. In
any and every circumstance, I
have learned the secret of facing
plenty and hunger, abundance
and need".* **Philippians 4:11-12**

The scripture in **Luke 12:15** admonishes us in this manner;

*"Take care, and be on your guard
against all covetousness, for one's
life does not consist in the
abundance of his possessions".*

Trying to covet what others have just so that we can have it too will incur long-term problems. Learning to appreciate and to be happy with what we have whether little or big is very important. It is not wrong to live a certain lifestyle. After all, who does not want to live well? But trying to live a life that will have long-term benefits for us is worth considering. If we as parents practice this, then it becomes easier to pass it on to our children.

I can remember vividly how many times I had to explain to my children that I had to fix things now so that I can leave some inheritance for them. We looked at TV programs such as "Pay It Or Lose It" where bailiffs would gain access into people's property to either seize their goods or evict them, mostly due to monies owed to the landlord, or to other companies. My children did not like the sight of it at all but thoy actually uscd to lovc thc program. I was happy they were able to see for themselves, which helped me whenever I spoke with them about finances.

I really do thank my Lord for my children, as I know they had some tough times by not getting that trainers or phones or the latest game when they wanted, but had to wait sometimes for the sale period to come round to get it a bit cheaper. I had to make such choices to avoid going back into the very hole I was trying to come out from. I did ensure that they still had some great times in the midst of it all. We would go out on our little breaks when we could afford it; dine out or watch a movie, or just give them a treat after working hard in school. I also managed to cater for their extra-curricular activities. All of these were done when conducive and not under any pressure for most of the time. To crown it all, we were still happy. We need to know that our happiness is not only based on the material things we have. Happiness can be holistic. We can all see that if we look around us, there are many people who have got what they want but are still not happy.

> *"But godliness with contentment is great gain. For we brought nothing into the world, and we can take nothing out of it. But if we have food and clothing, we will be content with*

*that. Those who want to get rich fall
into temptation and a trap and into
many foolish and harmful desires
that plunge people into ruin and
destruction. For the love of money is
a root of all kinds of evil. Some
people, eager for money, have
wandered from the faith and pierced
themselves with many griefs."*
1 Timothy 6:6-11

Some of the principles mentioned above can actually be applied to almost everyone reading this book despite its main focus on single parents. This is part of everyday life as we all go through this thing called life. Therefore, I am hoping we will reconsider, review and apply practical steps to experience a better standard of living.

I am also aware that some parents are very good at managing and planning so this might not necessary apply to that category of people, but will apply to most of us who need to improve in this area.

Also, in terms of individual financial status, outgoing dynamics can vary. Some parents might have inherited great fortunes and also re-invested so there is reproduction and therefore cash flow is never an issue. Planning is still necessary in each case.

Some parents might have received insurance from the loss of a loved one and have been able to also invest, and also been able to clear their debts so there is also the ease of cash flow. Some might have won the lottery or a cash competition referred to as quick money, and if planning is not done properly, one might end up losing everything.

However, as already mentioned, quite a lot of parents are struggling just to put a meal on the table for their children and battling with bills at the same time. With this in mind, it can be challenging to manage. The hard reality is that no one else is going to care about our future. We have to take matters into our own hands, and as harsh as that might seem, we might have to endure it anyways. I have been there, and am still going through some of these processes, and hoping for a better future. My recommendation will be, whatever stage we are at, let us do our best to manage. If we can manage our homes and families and personal lives, then we can manage others too and additional responsibilities given to us.

Lesson 3

I have also and am still learning to maintain my authority over my children and home in general. As a single parent, I discovered that I cannot afford to loosen my grip just because I love my children, or because their dad is no longer alive. Loosening my grip means losing control over them by:

- Letting them get away with whatever they want
- Refusing to discipline them because I do not want them to be upset with me and then play psychological games with me
- Seriously misbehaving when not giving in to their requests

The list goes on. These are very common occurrences, even amongst married couples and their children.

I am aware of the rights allotted to our children; therefore, I am not saying we give in totally to their demands without any form of reason. I believe there must be a balance when it comes to raising our children. Raising our children involves teaching, appraisal, love, care, compassion, mercy, discipline, inspiring, motivation and rebuke. The scriptures clearly tell us in **Proverbs** chapter **22 verse 6** that we must train our children in the way they should grow, so that when they are old enough, they will not depart from it. It is our duty as parents to manage our emotional issues as best as we can, obviously seeking out help and support where necessary, as we need to be strong mentally to fully support our children. I cannot say I am unable to control my children because it was their father that could do it perfectly, or another excuse such as, I am a single parent and life is hard, or I have to deal with more important things like bills and putting food on the table and so on. The truth is, those things have to be done but also the hard truth is every other thing has to be done alongside.

It is amazing how our children pick up things easily and the next thing is to start using those things against us as our weak points. They can be very smart and even talk about it sometimes amongst their peers about how strong or weak their parents are. I work with young people and it is amazing to see how they analyse issues regarding parenting. They are quite smarter than we think. They can also copy bad habits so easily which can be difficult to change. There is also that fine line that we should draw as parents and ensure it is not crossed. I learnt how important it is for us to first of all lead by example even before laying down our expectations. We show them love and they in turn abide by rules in the home. There has to be some boundaries, otherwise things will be chaotic. Some homes are ruled by the children as parents have been carried away by other personal distractions. There is complete lack of order and as a result some of this has translated to what we see on our streets and society in general. Our children should have respect for us no matter where we are at status wise.

I mentioned earlier in the previous chapter about some of the reasons why our children might rebel. It is mostly down to unbalanced disciplined where everything is extra militant. They go out of the home and it is surprising to see how they behave. They get back home and they look like angels. Another important factor is lack of love. I came from a background where parents provided everything they could for their children but no opportunity to interact on a one to one basis. We were told not to complain about things and just get on as long as things are taken care off. Well, I must remind us that times have changed. Parents must not only provide physically for their children, but provide for their emotional and help with social needs as well. It's all about being balanced. I am also aware that no matter what we do as parents, it can be frustrating and disappointing to see that sometimes our children chose to walk away into bad choices.

However, we cannot allow guilt to take over as long as we have a clear conscience that we have done our part. I also pray that as single parents, we will be strengthened mentally and physically to carry on and not give up by his grace.

Lesson 4

My fourth lesson learnt in this journey is; never to underestimate your value. Single fathers and mothers, know your worth. In my early years of single parenting, it felt like people didn't respect me I anymore. I had all these negative feelings about myself. Not that I did anything specific that would call for attention, but it just seemed to be like that. Low self-esteem would kick in every now and then; my confidence was lacking in so many areas. I was also a very shy person, which did not help at some point as all I needed to do was to speak to someone and seek wise counsel. Seeking help and receiving counsel from the right people that will help to motivate and encourage you is very important. These are the people that can see the greatness in you when you see nothing good in yourself or about your life. This therefore tells me that the company we keep can either help to make or break us. We often need to receive inspiration from others to take us to the next level, and surprisingly, others will be looking up to us for the same too whether we like it or not. We are impacting the lives of those around us and also in whatever sphere we find ourselves either positively or negatively. Our single parenthood is just a status and should not be a hindrance to positively impacting other lives.

We have all been blessed with several gifts and abilities, and it is also important to find out those abilities. **Romans 12:6-8** says:

> *"...we have different gifts, according to the grace given to each of us. If your gift is prophesying, then prophesy in accordance with your faith; if it is serving, then serve; if it is teaching, then teach; if it is to encourage, then give encouragement; if it is giving, then give generously; if it is to lead, do it diligently; if it is to show mercy, do it cheerfully."*

1 Corinthians 12:4-11

> *"There are different kinds of gifts, but the same Spirit distributes them. There are different kinds of service, but the same Lord. There are different kinds of working, but in all of them and in everyone it is the same God at work. Now to each one the manifestation of the Spirit is given for the common good. To one there is given through the Spirit a message of wisdom, to another a message of knowledge by means of the same*

*Spirit, to another faith by the same
Spirit, to another gifts of healing
by that one Spirit, to another
miraculous powers, to another
prophecy, to another
distinguishing between spirits, to
another speaking in different kinds
of tongues, and to still another the
interpretation of tongues. All these
are the work of one and the same
Spirit, and he distributes them to
each one, just as he determines."*

The majority of these come at no cost, and we can explore and utilise them to the best of our abilities. We can excel as we function in those areas. It shows we are all worth something to our families, friends, work colleagues and society in general. Some gifts can be natural and supernatural. Have we asked ourselves what gifts we have? These can be in the area plumbing, carpenter, electrician, hairdressing, makeup artistry, singing or music to mention but a few. Have some of us even identified our gifts? If so, are we already putting them to use? If not, why not? Do we believe that despite hindrances we can still do it? Especially by kicking out pride and accepting that we need help and counsel to get us there. Are we cheating ourselves by casting unnecessary blame on others or our status by feeling we are worth nothing? It is high time we take more responsibility for ourselves. **Philippians 4:13** is a widely quoted scripture "*I can do all things through Christ who strengthens me*".

We can still solve the problems of other people regardless of how we feel or where we are at. What we see as limitations in our lives can actually be an enlightenment to other people. The problem is we fail to value or do not acknowledge it at all. Instead we tend to look at other people's gifts. Not only that, we become jealous of them instead of finding inspiration. We lose complete touch of what our purpose is, and failure to act leads to contempt. I learnt to value what I had inside me. Some of my gifts that helped me meet the needs of others were hairdressing, cooking, childcare, pastoring, motivating and encouraging others with my life stories and testimonies. I remember way back in my days at university how I used to cook when my mates had parties. They used to call me a certain nickname "Mothers". I could cook very well as always ensured there was food in my room at all times when my mates came to visit. Caring is an extra grace I carry. It is a natural gift I have. Scripture clearly states that some have the gift of hospitality. It means many will be hospitable but some on another dimension. Feedback from individuals always encouraged me in this area. Little did I know that cooking would still be eminent in my life many years down the line. I met the needs of many through cooking, ranging from events to just families needing food at home. I can say I was valuable in this sense too. There were individuals who were only interested in my food and no one else's. Did I impact lives in this area too? I can say yes! I used the same principles when it came to hairdressing, making ladies and young girls look smart.

We all know how women place an emphasis on their hair. I would never forget how I used to go from family to family few years ago beautifying both mums and daughters. Sometimes people came to my house too. Funnily enough, hairdressing was part of my growing up. I used to do my neighbour' hair and that of family members and some school mates too, until I repeated my class in secondary school. Then my mum gave me a strict warning that I should refrain from touching anyone's head. Did I stop? Not at all. I was still doing it in hiding. She thought that was a distraction for me, and knowing how African parents thought then, values were never placed on these skills. It was all about going to school and university.

It becomes easier to look after other people's children once you have yours, and this is such a great gift we can give to other parents. The help you give to a parent by looking after their child means a whole lot to them. It keeps them free and available to do things quickly, or to go to work or even just taking time out. These are some of the meaningful forms of assistance we can render to the people around us.

I have been a Pastor for the past 3 years, but prior to this, I have served in leadership positions where I have had the opportunity to counsel people on a daily basis based on different life issues. Outside of ministry, I use my story to encourage others unashamedly. I also help with hosting and planning of events. Something I can do naturally as I just cannot afford to sit down to see someone's event be unsuccessful. I try to give my support as best as possible. I love to give genuine feedback to people as I always expect the same from others, and also for future improvement.

Most of these activities have taken place in my life despite my status. Was I going to sit down and not do anything because of my status? Did people question me on how I managed to do this in spite of my status? I would say sometimes yes and on other occasions no. What about the qualifying factor as a single woman and also a single parent? I would not say I experienced that personally. However, I have heard about other people's stories on how they were pulled down by some certain organisations for functioning as a single parent in a particular role, despite functioning excellently.

My suggestions would be to walk in boldness, believe in yourself and in your abilities, know that you are valuable in society and to family and friends. Appreciate the positive impact you have on others. Look at the bigger picture; that your status does not limit you though challenges come along. Above all, let your children see that you are a valuable asset to them. As parents, we should be the motivational drivers for our children, and be ready to encourage them too to start identifying their own gifts, talents and abilities. In this way, we are also helping them prepare for their future.

Lesson 5

I have also learnt to persevere in all things and not give up. It sounds easy saying it, but the application can be quite challenging. Failing to persevere actually tests our strengths and the length to which we can endure in life.

As a single parent, our children already know that they only have one parent. We all know how they try to manipulate us, or try their hard to break and bend rules. They try their hardest sometimes to push boundaries and sometimes successfully, or if not will keep trying.

As a parent, I had to maintain my stand. We have to keep on going whether they behave well at school or not, whether they get themselves into unnecessary trouble or not. We cannot afford to give up; they are children and they need that consistent guidance. They sometimes present themselves as mature, especially once they start puberty. They have mood swings; the tone with which they talk to us changes from soft to harsh. Getting them to do house chores or to tidy their rooms becomes a challenge. Some go through changes in their eating habits, some not wanting to socialise with family and sometimes even friends. I remember there were times when I got frustrated with the way my children would behave. But they were going through puberty which I failed to accept in the beginning. It took me a while to get to understand them and exercising a whole lot of patience on my part. As parents, we have to persevere through the failures and successes of our children. I also learnt to keep to my word. My 'yes' has to be yes, and my 'no' to be no. This was quite challenging at times but I had to persevere just so that the children were not confused. It can be quite easy for our children to figure out when we seem lost, or not handling things in the right way.

I also want to encourage us single mums and dads to persevere in achieving our own dreams and aspirations. Are you feeling bad for yourself about your dreams and aspirations that have been left dormant? Did you start the journey only to feel you could no longer continue due to challenges (especially looking after your children)? Have you asked yourself whether there is something you can start working on to bring that project back to life? I believe in the Tesco strap line that "every little helps". For me, it means making a little effort daily can have a big impact on that dream or project becoming a reality. We cannot afford to say that we will wait for things to be perfect in order for us to fulfil our dreams. Little drops of water make a mighty ocean indeed! Making that little time to take action makes a big difference. I am thinking about how I have gotten this far, and I can honestly say that there have been ups and downs.

I have had many dreams and projects that were incomplete for one reason or the other. Some were due to excuses that I should not have made looking back at things. On others, I gave up too quickly and just did not follow up. Should I have persevered more in the undone things? I believe so. But I only have to learn and move on. The scripture in **Isaiah 41:10** says:

> *"So do not fear, for I am with you;*
> *do not be dismayed for I am your*
> *God. I will strengthen you and help*

you; I will uphold you with my
righteous right hand".

Galatians 6:9 also is an encouragement for us.

> *"Let us not become weary in doing*
> *good, for at the proper time we will*
> *reap a harvest if we do not give*
> *up".*

Writing this book has really taught me that if one perseveres in their dream or project or vision, by the grace and strength of the Lord, and with the help and support of positive people around us, and also with our own self determination to see that project to the end no matter what, there will be a bountiful harvest. I just could not believe that I could write a book, and actually publish it. I looked at my life as a single parent, looked at others in the same position and the look of things in the society surrounding single parenthood, and decided that I could actually write a book on this. So the idea was there all along but I had to start with the planning, next the writing and the other formalities to follow. I was motivated on several occasions by my mentor and pastor who could see the good I did not see in myself, my lovely leaders around me in my church, some of my friends, colleagues and young people I have worked with. I had to be accountable as to how far I was with my writing whenever I was asked by anyone in the above mentioned categories. And not to forget my beloved children Franklyn and Doris who kept me on my toes to finish this book. I spent some long days and nights, and some of my holidays to help get to this point. Doing this and working full time was not a joke. But wow! If I can do it then you can definitely do it too.

The amazing grace of God helped me to persevere, and also gave me hope that there would be light at the end of the tunnel. I could actually visualise how people are going to read this book and be encouraged, or enlightened, and also review their way of thinking or judging on this topic of single parenting. The journey has not been easy, but I thank my Lord for the grace and strength to persevere. Could I do it all over again? I can boldly say 'yes'! Would yes have been my answer a few years ago? Absolutely not! But perseverance has taught me a lesson.

One day I was bold enough to ask my daughter about one thing she could say about me. I was surprised when she made a statement that was very true. I was weary at first as I try not to ask their opinion most times. Knowing how bold and outspoken they can be, I wanted to make sure I was ready for what they were going to say. But on this occasion, she really hit the nail on the head. She said to me; "I just like the way you handle things, and try to manage stuff even when it can be hard sometimes". She also said to me that I was strong. Hmmm! Remember I mentioned earlier about how our children notice things. It might seem sometimes that they do not care but they actually do. Unfortunately, they do not voice it out most times. I was actually impressed as she was completely accurate in what she said. Sometimes I do let them see me in my lowest moods, but yet still they see me rise up daily to keep pushing regardless.

CONCLUSION AND RECOMMENDATIONS

Writing this book has helped greatly in a way that I now think broadly about this subject. It has also enabled me to value and celebrate myself as a single parent, not allowing the opinion of others about my status hinder my progress in anyway. It has also given me more boldness to share my experiences to encourage as many that are in the same position as myself, both male and female single parents:

Firstly, to remind every single parent that you are not on your own, so do not be dismayed. Be encouraged! Challenge yourselves through the highs and the lows; do not give up even when it feels like it. Don't let the stigma of society push you into what you are not. You and I are unique in our own ways. Just try to do your best and have a clear conscience in yourselves first before trying to please others.

Secondly, whether we have messed up in the past or still do in the present, and feeling that we have failed in carrying out our roles in the lives of our children; Sadly we cannot go back to undo the past, but we can learn from those experiences to help us for the future so that we can produce a better result which will then bring a great outcome in the society. Let's not forget our roles at home transmits into the communities and society at large whether positively or negatively. As parents, let's continue to be examples to our children by giving daily motivation, encouragement and guidance as this is very vital. Also, looking for opportunities to develop ourselves against all odds will help contribute towards our confidence and self-worth, and also serve as role models for our children.

I encourage every single parent struggling to seek for immediate help and support where needed as "every little helps". Our wholeness is needed to enable us function properly. Let's remember we are doing the job of two parents.

I am also hoping that all organisations involved with families will continue do their best to support parents and their children for the good of all. When all entities work together, a greater positive impact is felt in the society at large.

I also encourage my readers to refrain from "quick to judge attitude". Every single parent cannot be put in the "same category" as situations surrounding them are completely different. Maybe, interacting a bit with single parents if possible can help unveil their stories which enable one to fully understand where they are coming from. This can also help to reduce the stigma surrounding single parenting.

Finally, I still do believe that it is a community that raises a child. Therefore, I encourage us all to get involve as much as we can in the lives of our young people, and support families and friends or neighbours as best as we can. I believe this will help to eradicate a lot of negativity we face in our communities and the society at large.

INSPIRATIONAL QUOTES FOR SINGLE PARENT MUMS AND DADS

"I can do all things through Christ who strengthens me." **Philippians 4:13**

"Don't be too harsh on yourself. Just do the best you can." Unknown

"Sometimes you have to forget what's gone, appreciate what still remains and look forward to what is coming." Anonymous

"Your children need your presence more than your presents-by"

Jesse Jackson

"Be the parent today that you want your kids to remember tomorrow." Unknown.

"Anytime you suffer a setback or disappointment, put your head down and plough ahead." Les Brown

"Butterflies don't know the colour of their wings, but human eyes know how beautiful it is. Likewise, you don't know how good you

are, but others can see that you are special.”

Linda Wooten

Printed in Great Britain
by Amazon

36799284R00067